SneakerBlossom

Study Guide

for

The Wanderings of Odysseus

by Rosemary Sutcliff

Answer-Key Edition

by Lisa Pelissier

www.sneakerblossom.com

Table of Contents

SneakerBlossom Study Guides are four things:

Christian, Classical, Versatile, Affordable

Christian: Every SneakerBlossom Study Guide functions not only as a guide to comprehension of the work being studied, but as a course in the Christian worldview.

Classical: SneakerBlossom Study Guides encourage students to study the great books of history in a manner appropriate to the student's capacity. Great emphasis is placed on contemplating virtue, truth, and beauty.

Versatile: SneakerBlossom Study Guides are available in many different formats that can be used from younger children through high school. They can be used in a homeschool setting or in a classroom setting.

Affordable: SneakerBlossom Study Guides can be used by the whole family. Purchase just the answer key and do the work aloud and you need only buy one book. Purchase a complete edition and use your own paper. Again, with only one book you have a study for the whole family.

SneakerBlossom Study Guides are available in several formats

Complete: Includes a section with comprehension and discussion questions at the front for the student(s) to use, and a section with comprehension and discussion questions and answers at the back for parents and teachers. Includes complete lists of Level A, Level B, and Level C character indexing and map work. If you can only afford one study guide, this is the one you want. This is the "use your own paper" or "do it out loud" version.

Answer Key: Includes all comprehension and discussion questions and answers. Also includes complete lists of Level A, Level B, and Level C character indexing and map work. This is the version to buy in order to grade the workbooks. You can also use the answer key if you are doing everything orally.

Relaxed Student Workbook: All comprehension questions are asked in a simple format, such as fill-in-the-blank or multiple choice. Character index is limited to main characters and well-known figures in Greek mythology. Map work is very general. (Level A) Discussion questions are not included.

Studious Student Workbook: All comprehension questions have lines for students to write answers. Character index lists main characters and minor characters. Map work is more specific. (Level B*) Discussion questions are not included.

Scholarly Student Workbook: All comprehension questions have lines for students to write answers. Discussion questions are included so that students can contemplate answers and write essays if desired. Character index includes every character mentioned in the text. Map work includes every place mentioned in the text. (Level C)

*In The Wanderings of Odysseus, Level B students use Level A mapwork.

SneakerBlossom Study Guides are easy to use.

1) <u>Read the Book:</u> Have the students read a chapter of the book, or read it to them.

2) <u>Comprehension Questions:</u> Answer the comprehension questions for each chapter. You can do this aloud with your students. You can purchase student workbooks and have your students do the work on their own. You can purchase the complete guide and have the students do the work on their own using a separate sheet of paper.

3) <u>Discussion Questions:</u> After comprehension questions are done, discuss one or more of the given topics with the students. Let the discussion be spontaneous and serendipitous. Don't feel that you need to address every discussion question given. If you have a good discussion then you've succeeded.

4) <u>Character Index:</u> A character index is given at the back of each student study guide as well as in the complete guide and the answer key. For each chapter read, students can fill out information in the index about the newly introduced characters in that chapter. They can use the index for reference as they read the book. The Character Index is leveled. **Never force anyone to do a Level C index. C is for CRAZY.** Some students will take great joy in recording information about every single character. For other students this will be torture. Do not torture them. It's there for the kids who find it a joyful exercise.

5) <u>Map Work:</u> Map work is included at the back of each study guide. For PDF versions of maps please email:

sneakerblossom@yahoo.com

Additional Thoughts

Comprehension Questions

     In my opinion, comprehension questions exist to help the child remember what they read, and also to help the teacher verify that the child has read the material. It is up to you whether or not you require the answers in complete sentences. If you have a child that always remembers everything they read, just read and discuss: don't bother with comprehension questions at all. It's up to you. Your goal is not the make your child memorize the contents of the text. Your goal is to make your child love learning. A child who loves learning becomes an adult who continues learning over the course of his or her life. Your goal should be to help your child love God and to live a life full of virtue, truth, and beauty. Use the book and the SneakerBlossom Study Guides in your efforts toward that end.

Discussion Questions

     Please note that my answers to discussion questions are only a starting place. They are not "the right answer". Your discussions may take an entirely different path.

Introduction: What is the *Odyssey?*

The Wanderings of Odysseus by Rosemary Sutcliff is a retelling of the classic tale, the *Odyssey*. The *Odyssey* was written by Homer, an ancient Greek poet. It is generally considered to be one of the first works of Western literature, written in the 8th century BC. The *Odyssey* tells the story of Odysseus' return home after the Trojan War.

Homer also wrote the *Iliad*, which tells the story of a brief segment of the Trojan War. Virgil wrote the *Aeneid*, which tells the story of the Trojan Aeneas' journey as he left a fallen Troy and sought to establish a new city, which became Rome. The story of the Trojan horse is part of the *Aeneid*.

The *Iliad*, the *Odyssey*, and the *Aeneid* are foundational works to ancient Greek and Roman culture and to all of Western civilization.

Prologue

Characters Introduced in this Chapter

Level A: Odysseus

Level B: Agamemnon, Helen, Menelaus, Paris

Map Work:

Level A: Greece, Ithaca, Troy

Level C: Sparta

Comprehension Questions and Answers

Q1: Why did the Greeks fight the Trojans in the Trojan War?

Prince Paris of Troy had taken King Menelaus' wife, Helen.

Agamemnon, a Greek king, gathered all the Greeks to go

conquer Troy and get Helen back.

Q2: What good idea did Odysseus have that helped the Greeks win

the war?

Odysseus devised the Trojan Horse. Warriors were hidden

inside an enormous statue of a horse. They were smuggled

into the city, only to attack it in the night.

Q3: Who won the Trojan War?

The Greeks.

Q4: What is this book going to be about?

This book is about Odysseus' journey home from Troy after

the Trojan War.

Chapter 1: The Sacker of Cities

<u>Characters Introduced in this Chapter</u>

Level B: Apollo

Level C: Maron, Maron's wife, Maron's child

<u>Map Work</u>

Level A: Ismarus (Thrace), Island of the Lotus Eaters

<u>Comprehension Questions and Answers</u>

Q1: Where did Odysseus first stop with his ships?

Thrace.

Q2: What did Odysseus and his men do there? Why?

Odysseus and his men attacked and plundered the city of
Ismarus. The Thracians were allies of Troy and he still
considered them enemies.

Q3: Whom did Odysseus spare?

Odysseus spared Maron, a priest of Troy, and his wife and
child.

Q4: Why did Odysseus and his men flee from the Thracians?

The Thracians attacked them in the night while they were
"woolly-witted" from eating and drinking so much. Over
seventy men were killed as they ran for their ships.

Q5: Where did they go next?

> *After a nine-day long storm, they landed on the shore of the*
> *island of the lotus-eaters.*

Q6: What happened to those who ate the fruit of the island?

> *They lost all knowledge of the past and the future. They lost*
> *the will to do anything. They just wanted to lay around*
> *dreaming happy dreams.*

Q7: What was the name of the stupor-inducing plant?

> *The lotus.*

Suggested Lines of Discussion to Pursue

DQ1: The text does not give a reason, but why do you think that
Odysseus spared Maron and his family?

> *Maron was a priest of Apollo and the keeper of a sacred*
> *laurel grove. Odysseus would not have wanted to anger the*
> *gods by hurting a priest or a sacred grove.*

DQ2: Did the Thracians attack Odysseus and his men justly?

> *Odysseus and his men attacked them first. Then they rested*
> *on the beach eating the Thracians' cattle and drinking their*
> *wine. The Thracians seem justified in attacking Odysseus*
> *and his men.*

DQ3: The men who ate the lotus fruit were happy. Why did Odysseus call them worthless and force them to go back to the ship?

This speaks to the idea of what it means to be human. The men who ate the lotus fruit and the inhabitants of the island were happy, but they were happy in the way that an animal is happy when its belly is full and it is physically comfortable. The human soul is much more intricate than that. Man is made in the image of God. To waste away a life sitting and eating and being content is not enough. Man was created to glorify God, and to experience and participate in truth, beauty, and goodness. He cannot comprehend any of those things while his mind sleeps in a dreamy, animalistic state.

Chapter 2: The Cyclops

Characters Introduced in this Chapter

> Level A: Cyclopes, Poseidon, Zeus
>
> Level C: Laertes, Polyphemus

Map Work

> Level A: Land of the Cyclopes

Comprehension Questions and Answers

Q1: When they came to a new island, why did Odysseus think it was inhabited?

> *Odysseus could see fires in the distance and he could hear sheep.*

Q2: Who lived on the island? Who was their father?

> *The Cyclopes lived on the island. Poseidon was their father.*

Q3: Why didn't Odysseus leave the cave before the owner came back? Why couldn't he and his men leave afterward?

> *Before the cyclops came, Odysseus wanted to find out who the owner of the cave was. When he arrived, the cyclops set a large flat stone against the doorway and they could not escape.*

Q4: Why didn't Odysseus kill the cyclops while he slept?

> *Odysseus needed the cyclops to remove the stone blocking the entrance to the cave. If he killed the cyclops, he and his men would be trapped.*

Q5: What does Odysseus tell the cyclops his name is?

Nobody.

Q6: How did the men get past the cyclops and out of the cave?

They hung onto the bellies of the sheep as the sheep went out to pasture. The blinded cyclops could not see them or feel them and so they escaped.

Suggested Lines of Discussion to Pursue

DQ1: Why does Odysseus tell the cyclops his name as he is sailing away? Do you think this was wise?

Odysseus is proud of tricking the cyclops. He wants the cyclops to know how clever he has been. This was unwise and it negatively affected the rest of his journey. The cyclops pronounced a curse on Odysseus once he knew his name, calling on his father, the god Poseidon, to carry it out.

DQ2: Do you think Odysseus' pride will end up hurting him? Will Polyphemus' prophecy come true?

Answers will vary.

We learn, though, that the ancient Greeks expected the gods to take an active role in the lives of humans. First Odysseus spares Maron, the priest of Apollo. He doesn't want to offend the gods and bring trouble on himself. Here we learn that Polyphemus fully expects his father, Poseidon, to avenge the wrong done to him.

Chapter 3: The Lord of the Winds

Characters Introduced in this Chapter

      Level B: Aeolus

Map Work

      Level A: Aeolus' Island, Land of the Giants

Comprehension Questions and Answers

Q1: What gift did Aeolus give Odysseus?

Aeolus gave Odysseus a bag containing all the winds of the world except one. The one, a gentle wind, was to drive his ships home.

Q2: What warning does Aeolus give them about the gift?

Aeolus tells them not to open the bag until they are safely harbored at Ithaca.

Q3: How did the bag get opened? What happened because of it?

Odysseus fell asleep in sight of home. The men opened the bag, thinking it was treasure that Odysseus was trying to keep for himself. The released winds drove them back to Aeolus' island.

Q4: Why does Aeolus refuse to help them again?

Aeolus believes that their misfortune occurred because the gods hate them. He doesn't want to side with anyone the gods hate.

Q5: Why does Odysseus keep his own ship out of the harbor when they arrive at their next stop?

Odysseus was still angry with his men for releasing the winds and wants to punish them.

Q6: Who lives on the island? What is their reaction to Odysseus and his men?

Giants live on the island. They kill the first man to reach them and cast rocks from the cliffs to destroy the rest of the ships and men.

Q7: How many ships full of men are lost? How many escape?

Eleven ships full of men are lost. Only Odysseus' ship escapes.

Q8: Why does Odysseus believe this tragedy has come upon him?

Odysseus believes that Poseidon has heard the prayer of the cyclops and has set his face against him.

Suggested Lines of Discussion to Pursue

DQ1: Why was a bag of wind a good gift for Odysseus?

This was a good gift: with all the fiercer winds imprisoned in the bag, it would be easy for them to get back to Ithaca.

DQ2: Discuss: Aeolus refuses to offer charitable help because it might offend the gods. Is it always appropriate to offer charitable help? Why or why not?

> *In the Bible it is clear that, as a general principle, Christians are to offer charity even to their enemies. There are other times in the Bible where believers refused help to their enemies. Jael invites a fleeing Sisera into her tent and then kills him. She is lauded by Deborah for doing the work of God. But this was not a personal killing, but a wartime killing on behalf of Israel. The Christian, as an individual, is instructed to extend charity to all.*

Chapter 4: The Enchantress

Characters Introduced in this Chapter

Level A: Circe

Level B: Hermes

Level C: Eurylochus

Map Work

Level A: Circe's Island

Comprehension Questions and Answers

Q1: Whom does Odysseus send to find the inhabitants of the latest island at which they land?

Odysseus divides the crew into two groups, one under the leadership of Eurylochus, and another under his own. They draw lots to decide which crew will explore the island, and Eurylochus' group goes.

Q2: What happened to the men Eurylochus was leading?

They drank wine from a strange woman, who turned them into pigs.

Q3: What help does Hermes give Odysseus?

Hermes gives Odysseus a magic potion that makes him impervious to Circe's wine and wand. He advises him how to release his men from the spell.

Q4: Why didn't Odysseus take his ship and flee from Circe's island
when he had the chance?

Odysseus is hungry for strange experiences.

Suggested Lines of Discussion to Pursue

DQ1: Is Circe a better host than Polyphemus?

*Circe's initial response to the presence of strangers on her
island was to turn them into pigs. She would have done the
same to Odysseus had he not held Hermes' flower. She was
not a hospitable host. It can be argued, however, that she
was a better host than Polyphemus: she didn't eat any of
her guests.*

DQ2: Hermes picks a magical plant to protect Odysseus. The text
says "It was a plant which cannot be picked by mortal men; but to
the gods all things are easy." Are all things easy for the Greek gods?
What about the God of the Bible?

*If "easy" means that great feats can be performed with little
effort, then both the Greek gods and the God of the Bible
are said to be endowed with that power. But not all things
are easy for the gods. The Greek gods fight among
themselves. They can be injured. They can be thwarted.
The God of the Bible cannot be injured or thwarted and He
does not fight "among Himself". But God's heart can be
grieved by the actions of His people. That is not "easy".*

Chapter 5: The Land of the Dead

Characters Introduced in this Chapter

>Level A: Hades, Penelope, Persephone

>Level B: Tiresias

>Level C: Achilles, Ajax, Elpenor, Hyperion, Odysseus' mother,

>>Minos, Orion, Sisyphus, Tantalus

Map Work

>Level A: Land of the Dead, Thrinacia

>Level C: Oceanus River

Comprehension Questions and Answers

Q1: How long did Odysseus and his men stay with Circe?

>*A year.*

Q2: What does Circe tell Odysseus he must do if he wants to get
home?

>*Circe tells Odysseus to go to the Land of the Dead and*
>*consult with Tiresias of Thebes, a ghostly, blind prophet.*

Q3: Who is the first ghost Odysseus meets? What is his request?

>*The first ghost to approach is Elpenor, the young sailor who*
>*died just before they left Circe's island. He begs Odysseus to*
>*burn his body so he can commune with the other ghosts.*

Q4: Who is the second ghost Odysseus meets?

>*The second ghost is Odysseus' mother.*

Q5: What does the ghost of Tiresias have to do in order to have

enough strength to talk with Odysseus?

Tiresias has to drink the blood of the sheep Odysseus and his

men have sacrificed, in order to gain strength from it.

Q6: What advice does Tiresias offer?

Tiresias says the only way they have a chance to come home

safely is to leave the cattle of Hyperion alone when they

encounter them.

Q7: How did Agamemnon die?

Agamemnon was killed by his wife's lover as soon as he got

home from the Trojan War.

Suggested Lines of Discussion to Pursue

DQ1: Compare and contrast the Land of the Dead with the Christian

beliefs about Heaven and Hell.

Heaven is where God dwells. The final destination for those

who hope in Christ will be the new earth, remade in

perfection, free from the sin and destruction to which it is

now bound. Hell is a place of torment reserved for the devil,

demons, and those who reject Christ.

By contrast, the Land of the Dead is the final

destination for all of the Greeks. It is a physical place:

Odysseus and his men go there by boat. It is not possible to get to the Christian Hell by boat. Some of the Greeks are tormented in the Land of the Dead. The Land of the Dead (Hades) also includes a pleasant land for those who pleased the gods (the Elysian Fields).

DQ2: Should Christians believe in ghosts? Do modern people believe in ghosts? How are modern beliefs in ghosts similar to the beliefs of the ancient Greeks? How are they different?

Christians believe in spirits. Every person has a spirit and a body. During a person's lifetime, the spirit and body act as one unit. Death happens when the spirit and the body split apart. Christians also believe in demons. Demons are angelic beings who have decided not to serve God.

Some modern people believe that the spirits of people who have died are floating around earth, communicating with people who are still alive. Many people do not believe in this kind of ghost. Many people do not believe that humans have souls at all.

The ancient Greeks believed that the Land of the Dead was for the souls of the dead. Those souls were ghosts. This is similar to both the Christian and the modern beliefs that ghosts are the souls of humans. The ghosts cannot enter the Land of the Dead unless their physical body is burned. The ancient Greek ghosts taste the blood of the sacrifice. This seems to indicate that they have some sort of physical body, unlike the Christian soul or the modern ghost.

Chapter 6: Sea Perils

Characters Introduced in this Chapter

> Level A: Charybdis, Sirens, Scylla

> Level B: Calpyso

Map Work

> Level A: Calypso's Island, Sirens' Island, Strait of Scylla and

> > Charybdis, Wandering Rocks

> Level C: Olympus

Comprehension Questions and Answers

Q1: Where did Odysseus go first after he left the land of the dead?
What did he do there?

> *Odysseus went back to Circe's island in order to burn the*

> *body of Elpenor.*

Q2: What do the Sirens do to sailors?

> *The Sirens lure sailors with their sweet singing. Their singing*

> *sucks the souls out of men.*

Q3: How do they avoid the peril of the Sirens?

> *The men plug their ears with wax so they can't hear the*

> *Sirens' singing. Odysseus wants to hear them, so he has the*

> *men tie him to the mast until they are past the danger.*

Q4: What is Charybdis?

> *Charybdis is a sea-monster who sucks up the sea three times*

> *a day and then vomits it out again. This creates an*

inescapable whirlpool.

Q5: What is Scylla?

> *Scylla is a six-headed monster who lives on a cliffside. She*
>
> *has long scary teeth and she eats anything that passes by.*

Q6: What are the Wandering Rocks?

> *The Wandering Rocks are reefs that are not bound to the*
>
> *seafloor. They smash anything that passes between them.*

Q7: Why does Odysseus choose to pass by Scylla rather than
Charybdis?

> *Scylla can only eat six men at a time, while Charybdis can*
>
> *take down the whole ship.*

Q8: When Odysseus goes off to pray, what do his men do?

> *They eat the cattle of Hyperion.*

Q9: What happens as a result of the theft of the cattle?

> *All of the men except Odysseus are killed in a storm.*

Suggested Lines of Discussion to Pursue

DQ1: Was it foolish of Odysseus to listen to the Sirens' song? Or
was it an admirable display of bravery and curiosity? How can we
tell the difference between bravery and foolishness?

> *We have seen throughout the book that Odysseus will take*
>
> *risks for the sake of adventure. It is not unexpected that he*

would refuse the wax for his ears and want to listen to the Sirens. If he had complete trust in his men, then perhaps it was not foolish to assume he could listen without harm. And his men proved true: they did not untie him until the danger was past. But it is conceivable that the men would have listened to his pleas to be untied. If they had freed him he would have died. It was a huge risk with no fitting reward.

A fool does not consider the consequences of his actions. He may do the same deed as the brave man, but without considering the cost to himself or those around him. A brave man understands the danger inherent in his act. He chooses to act despite the danger in order to obtain some greater good, like victory in battle, or saving a life. A brave man is afraid: a fool is not.

DQ2: Was Odysseus right to sacrifice six men to the jaws of six-headed Scylla in order to avoid the entire ship being swallowed by Charybdis?

It seems that he didn't have any other choice if he wanted to get back home. They had to pass that part of the sea. They had to risk one monster or the other. Odysseus chose the monster that would spare the most lives.

Chapter 7: Telemachus Seeks His Father

Characters Introduced in this Chapter

> Level A: Athene, Telemachus
>
> Level B: Eurycleia
>
> Level C: Mentes, Nestor, Pisistratus, Proteus

Map Work

> Level C: Africa, Cyprus, Egypt, Ethiopia, Libya, Nile River (not
>
> on map), Pharos (not on map), Phoenicia, Pylos,
>
> Same

Comprehension Questions and Answers

Q1: How long does Odysseus stay with Calypso? Why?

Odysseus stays with Calypso for seven years. He doesn't
have the means to build and staff a ship by himself and
Calypso won't help him because she is in love with him and
wants him to stay.

Q2: Why has Penelope's palace been invaded by young men?

The young men see the lack of leadership in Ithaca, with
Odysseus gone, his father Laertes retired to the country, and
Telemachus only a boy. They think that if they can get
Penelope to marry one of them, they can seize the kingdom.

Q3: What does Athene tell Telemachus?

Athene tells Telemachus that his father is alive and on his
way home.

Q4: What does Telemachus do?

> *First Telemachus tries to take charge of the city and fails.*
>
> *Then he sets out to sea to talk to his father's allies, Nestor*
>
> *and Menelaus.*

Q5: What information does Menelaus give Telemachus? How did he learn it?

> *Menelaus tells Telemachus that Odysseus had been held*
>
> *captive by the nymph Calypso on her island for seven years.*
>
> *He learned this by demanding news of his friends from the*
>
> *Old Man of the Sea.*

Suggested Lines of Discussion to Pursue

DQ1: Odysseus stayed for seven years with Calpyso, who was in love with him. Do you think he loved her back?

> *Seven years is a long time to spend waiting to go home. He*
>
> *must have developed a fondness for Calpyso. But the book is*
>
> *clear that all the time he was longing for home and for his*
>
> *wife.*

DQ2: In the first six chapters of this book, every character on the ships dies except Odysseus. At the end of chapter seven, Menelaus declares that the gods have gone to great pains to keep Odysseus alive. What do we learn about the Greek gods from this? Compare the Greek gods to the God of the Bible.

The Greek gods caused a lot of trouble for Odysseus and his men. In Chapter 3, Poseidon sees to it that 11 of the 12 ships are destroyed and the men killed. In Chapter 6, Hyperion does away with Odysseus' remaining companions. The Greek gods seem particularly bloodthirsty, especially, since, in Chapter 3, at least, the person that Poseidon was angry with was Odysseus, who lived, not the men who died.

From this we can surmise that the Greek gods viewed people in a more collective way than as individuals. They didn't kill this man and that man, they killed Odysseus' men. The God of the Bible does demonstrate a more communal view of humankind than the one we are used to. In the Old Testament, he often punishes Israel as a whole, even though not every Israelite had turned to idols. In the New Testament we see whole families being baptized at once. But we also see in the Bible, that God treats people as individuals. We see him sparing Lot and his family, taking them out of Sodom before its destruction. He saved Noah through the flood that destroyed the rest of humankind. And He tells us that He has written our names in the Book of Life. He knows us as individuals.

Chapter 8: Farewell to Calypso

Characters Introduced in this Chapter

>   Level C: Ino

Comprehension Questions and Answers

Q1: What message did Hermes bring to Calypso?

>   *Hermes tells Calypso that she must let Odysseus go home.*

Q2: What gift did Odysseus refuse to receive from Calypso?

>   *Immortality.*

Q3: How long does it take Odysseus to build a boat once Calypso gives him the materials?

>   *Four days.*

Q4: What problems does Odysseus have on his sea voyage?

>   *Poseidon causes a storm to wreck Odysseus' ship, and Odysseus' heavy clothing, a gift from Calypso, drags him down.*

Q5: Who rescues Odysseus? How?

>   *A sea goddess, Ino, gives Odysseus her veil in place of his heavy clothing. The veil can keep him from harm.*

Q6: Which gods are working against Odysseus? Which gods are acting on his behalf?

>   *Poseidon and Hyperion are against him. In this chapter, Hermes, Ina, and Athene help him. Calypso was holding Odysseus on her island against his will, but upon the*

command of Hermes, assists him to get home.

Suggested Lines of Discussion to Pursue

DQ1: The books talks about Hermes and how he "bound his winged sandals to his feet". Would you feel more comfortable with wings on your feet, like Hermes, or wings on your shoulders or arms, like birds and insects, or with winged fingers, like bats? Why?

> *Answers will vary. Personally I think it would be difficult to balance on winged shoes while flying through the air. I would like to have shoulder wings, separate from my arms, so that I can use my arms for different things.*

DQ2: What is immorality? Where does it come from in the book? How is this different than the eternal life promised to followers of Jesus?

> *Immortality means the inability to die. To the Greeks, it was the possession of the gods, and sometimes of the half-gods, like Achilles, who was immortal except for his heel. Calpyso, a nymph, declares that she had the ability to offer it to Odysseus. When Christians reference eternal life, it means life in the next world in new bodies, a life which begins with spiritual rebirth in Jesus. The Christian God is immortal, and so are angels and demons, because they are not bodily creatures and cannot die.*

DQ3: Calypso would have made Odysseus immortal if he had let her. Why did he choose a mortal life? Would you choose immortality if you could?

> *In opting for mortality, Odysseus chooses his life with Penelope over an immortal life with Calypso. It was an act of love toward his wife, and a choice to be who he was: a man and not a god.*

Chapter 9: The King's Daughter

Characters Introduced in this Chapter

>Level B: Artemis, Nausicaa

>Level C: Alcinous, Arete

Map Work

>Level A: Phaeacia

>Level C: Delos

Comprehension Questions and Answers

Q1: Why did Nausicaa go to the river?

>*Nausicaa goes to the river to wash her clothes, bidden to do*
>
>*so by Athene disguised as her friend while she slept.*

Q2: Where is Odysseus when Nausicaa and her friends are playing and washing clothes at the river?

>*Odysseus is sleeping in the bushes.*

Q3: Why are Nausicaa's friends afraid of Odysseus?

>*He was stark naked. His hair was matted and he was*
>
>*covered with sea salt. His feet were bloody. He was a mess.*

Q4: What does Nausicaa tell Odysseus to do? Why?

>*Nausicaa tells Odysseus to follow her and the maidens to the*
>
>*city's edge. Then he is to wait for a while before entering the*
>
>*city and coming to the palace. Nausicaa is afraid of what her*
>
>*father will say if the whole city sees her bringing home a*
>
>*strange man.*

Q5: How does Athene help Odysseus get to the palace?

> *Athene puts a mist of unseeing around him so that no one will see him walking through the city.*

Q6: How do King Alcinous and Queen Arete receive Odysseus?

> *They show him hospitality, giving him food and shelter. The king offers him a ship and rowers to help him get home.*

Suggested Lines of Discussion to Pursue

DQ1: Throughout this chapter we see Athene guiding Odysseus, from the vision she grants to Nausicaa, to manipulating the girls' ball game so that they find Odysseus, to providing him with a concealing mist for his journey through the city. Ought we, as Christians, to expect our God to provide for us in this manner?

> *I believe that God does provide for us in this manner. There are examples in the Bible as well as throughout history that show that God takes an active role in the happenings among humans. We can look at many examples of God's participation in human history: the creation of Adam and Eve, the commission of Noah to build the ark, the callings of Abraham and of Samuel, the conversion of Paul, etc.*
>
> *Colossians 1:16-17 says "For by Him all things were created, both in the heavens and on earth, visible and*

invisible, whether thrones or dominions or rulers or

authorities—all things have been created through Him and

for Him. He is before all things, and in Him all things hold

together." God is in charge of the earth an all that is in it.

But in terms of our expectations, we should keep in

mind that like Odysseus, we can't always see the hand of

God in our circumstances. Two of the instances of guidance

in this chapter were given to characters other than

Odysseus. In the third example, Athene appears to Odysseus

in disguise: he doesn't know it's she. While we certainly

ought not extrapolate Christian theology from a retelling of

the Odyssey, *the example provided is a good picture of how*

the hand of God provides for us.

DQ2: Why doesn't Odysseus tell the king and queen his name?

Nobody asked him.

DQ3: Nausicaa asks Odysseus to lag behind her so that her father
won't be upset with her for bringing a strange man with her
through the city. But when the king criticizes Nausicaa for not
bringing him home directly, Odysseus lies and says that it was his
idea to lag behind. Why does he lie? Was it right for him to lie?

Odysseus lies in order to be kind to Nausicaa. He doesn't want her father to blame her for not bringing him directly to the palace. His lie was a chivalrous lie, meant to lift the princess above her father's criticism: a "little white lie". God is the Truth. Lies don't glorify God. But in the ethic of ancient Greece, it would have been acceptable. Their gods lied when it served their purposes and would not have looked down on Odysseus for his cunning or his chivalry.

Chapter 10: The Phaeacian Games

Characters Introduced in this Chapter

Level B: Aphrodite, Ares

Level C: Euryalus, Laodamas

Comprehension Questions and Answers

Q1: What is the topic of the blind bard's song?

The blind bard sings of the heroes of Troy.

Q2: Why are the young men mocking Odysseus?

Odysseus did not participate in their games. They suggest he
is a weakling, despite his muscular build.

Q3: What skill do the young people of Phaeacia demonstrate that
impresses Odysseus?

They do a dance with a shining ball, which they toss in the
air between them as they dance.

Q4: What topic does the bard choose for his song during the feast?
What is Odysseus' response?

The bard sings the song of the final defeat of Troy and of
Odysseus' role in creating the Trojan horse. Odysseus is
grieved and weeps.

Q5: Why are the people shocked when Odysseus tells them who he
is?

They have heard many songs about the great Odysseus. He
is a legend to them, someone almost unreal.

Q6: What does Alcinous request from Odysseus? What is Odysseus'
response?

>*Alcinous asks Odysseus to tell his story. Odysseus complies.*

Suggested Lines of Discussion to Pursue

DQ1: The author says that the gods made the bard sightless on
purpose, so that he would sing more sweetly. Does the God of the
Bible make people blind on purpose?

>*In John 9, Jesus comes upon a blind man. The disciples ask*
>*Jesus whether it was due to the man's sin or to his parents'*
>*sin that he is blind. Jesus tells them that it happened so that*
>*the works of God might be displayed in him. He does not*
>*specify that God is the one who caused the blindness, only*
>*that God allowed the blindness in order that He might be*
>*glorified through the man's healing. The ailments of man are*
>*the result of sin on God's creation.*

>*We also see in the book of Acts, that God blinds Saul*
>*temporarily upon his conversion. This also showed forth the*
>*glory of God.*

DQ2: Did the hospitality of Alcinous and Arete change once they found out who Odysseus was? Did they act morally?

Their hospitality was marvelously complete before they knew Odysseus' identity. They had already given him a gold cup, a mantle and tunic that the queen had woven, and many other gifts, as well as providing the ships to carry him home. The Bible tells Christians to treat others without partiality; to treat people well regardless of whether they are rich or poor. Alcinous and Arete are a good example of this kind of hospitality.

Chapter 11: Return to Ithaca

<u>Characters Introduced in this Chapter</u>

Level B: Eumaeus

<u>Map Work</u>

Level C: Crete

<u>Comprehension Questions and Answers</u>

Q1: What did Odysseus do on the journey back to Ithaca?

He slept.

Q2: Why does Athene put a mist over the land?

Athene doesn't want Odysseus to know he is home until she has time to warn him of the dangers he will face.

Q3: Why can't Odysseus just go home?

In the palace, 108 suitors are clamoring for the hand of his wife, Penelope.

Q4: What two things does Athene help Odysseus do before she goes to fetch Telemachus?

She changes his appearance to that of a beggar and she helps him hide the treasures that he was given by the Phaeacians.

Q5: Where is Telemachus?

At the home of Menelaus and Helen.

Q6: How does Odysseus know that the man who comes to the swineherd's house is his son?

Telemachus looks just like Odysseus and his father, Laertes.

Q7: What plan to Odysseus and Telemachus devise?

They plan that Odysseus shall go to the palace disguised as a beggar. Telemachus was to hide the weapons and shields of the suitors.

Suggested Lines of Discussion to Pursue

DQ1: What would it be like to live in a world where multiple gods had different fates planned for you? Poseidon was using his supernatural powers to thwart Odysseus. Athene was using hers to help him. How would is this different from the way you relate to God as a Christian?

It would be really confusing to have to please many gods at the same time. Their demands may be quite varied and may even conflict. There may be gods you don't even know about that can get angry with you. In the Bible we see this desperate need to please the gods in Acts 17:23. Paul acknowledges an altar that the Romans have built that was dedicated to an unknown god, the god they didn't know about. Living without understanding the requirements needed to keep supernatural beings from turning against you would be a wearisome kind of life. The God of the Bible is One, and He loves His creatures. His standard for us is His own perfection: a perfection we can never attain. But in his love and mercy, God provided Jesus to us to fulfill the perfection of the law in our place. We can have rest for our souls, a rest that those who worshipped the Greek gods could never have, knowing that God loves us and has covered our sins with the blood of His Son.

Chapter 12: The Beggar in the Corner

Characters Introduced in this Chapter

> Level B: Argus

> Level C: Eurymachus, Irus, Melanthius, Melantho

Comprehension Questions and Answers

Q1: Who is the first to recognize Odysseus, despite his beggar's costume?

> *His old dog, Argus.*

Q2: Why were the other suitors nervous when Antinous struck Odysseus with a stool?

> *An unknown person might be a god in disguise. Antinous should have known better than to strike a stranger.*

Q3: Why did Irus fight with Odysseus?

> *The beggar, Irus, demands to fight Odysseus for the privilege of being the only beggar at the palace.*

Q4: Who asks Odysseus about his identity?

> *Penelope.*

Q5: Who was the second to recognize the beggar as Odysseus? What made her sure it was he?

> *Odysseus' old nurse, Eurycleia, recognizes Odysseus by a scar on his leg.*

Q6: What contest does Odysseus suggest? What is to be the prize?

> *Odysseus suggests an archery contest. The winner will wed*
> *Penelope.*

<u>Suggested Lines of Discussion to Pursue</u>

DQ1: Melanthius, the royal goatherd, supports the suitors over
Telemachus in the race to be king in Odysseus' place. He does this
because he wants to win the favor of whichever suitor becomes
king, in the hope that the new king will be generous to him. Is this a
noble way to behave? Why or why not?

> *Melanthius acts from selfish motives: he wants to be favored*
> *by the new king. If he thought Telemachus were more likely*
> *to become king than any of the suitors, he would have*
> *supported Telemachus. This tells us that he is not acting*
> *according to well-reasoned beliefs about who was the*
> *rightful heir to the throne, but is willing to set aside any*
> *beliefs he has on that topic for the sake of gain. He gives up*
> *his personhood for money.*
>
> *In the Bible there are numerous examples of prophets*
> *who risked danger and endured hardship for the sake of*
> *delivering a message the king did not like. Truth is more*
> *important that flattering someone in order to get something*
> *from them.*

DQ2: Have you ever had a pet with the kind of loyalty that Argus demonstrated toward Odysseus? Talk about it.

Answers will vary.

DQ3: The suitors were uneasy because Antinous abused a beggar: they knew a beggar could be a god in disguise. Does Christianity support this idea? Should the poor be treated well because of what they might turn out to be?

Hebrews 13:2 says "Do not forget to show hospitality to strangers, for by so doing some people have shown hospitality to angels without knowing it." (NIV). The Bible clearly insists that the Christian keep in mind that people are not always what they seem, and supports the idea of treating them well because of it.

In other places, however, the Christian is instructed to treat everyone well, not because they might be angels, but because they are made in the image of God, and share a common humanity. (James 2:1-9).

In summary, yes, a stranger may be an angel in disguise, but it may be only a human made in the image of God. It is necessary to treat everyone with love.

DQ4: If the Greek gods could disguise themselves as humans, and angels in the Bible can disguise themselves as humans, does it follow that the Greek gods are angels or demons (fallen angels)?

In Psalm 106:34-38, the Bible equates the pagan idols of Canaan with demons (NASB & ESV; devils in KJV; "false gods" in NIV). Deuteronomy 32: 16-17 equates false gods with demons (same translations as above). I Corinthians 10:20 also says that the gods to whom the pagans offer sacrifices are demons (NIV agrees with the translation "demon" in this instance). It is apparent that Biblically, the pagan gods can be real beings: they are demons.

Is it possible that some of them were not demons, but were just made up entities? Of course. But this does not detract from the idea that demons actually do masquerade as gods, stealing worship from mankind that should have gone to the true God.

Chapter 13: The Archery Contest

Characters Introduced in this Chapter

Level C: Ctesippus, Echetus, Eurynome, Philoetius

Comprehension Questions and Answers

Q1: What sign does Odysseus receive that he has the favor of Zeus?

A clap of thunder from the clear sky assures him of Zeus' favor.

Q2: What prophecy is given to the suitors?

A servant who is a seer predicts their deaths.

Q3: Who sets up the archery contest? What does he do next?

Telemachus sets up the axes and tries to string his father's bow. He fails.

Q4: Whom does Odysseus recruit to help him? What do they do?

Odysseus recruits Eumaeus, the shepherd, and Philoetius, the cowherd. They lock the suitors in the hall so they can't escape.

Q5: What happens when Odysseus takes up the bow and arrow?

He strings it easily and shoots the arrow through the twelve rings.

<u>Suggested Lines of Discussion to Pursue</u>

DQ1: At the beginning of the chapter, Odysseus asks for a sign of Zeus' favor and is given one. Is it appropriate for Christians to pray for a sign? Does God work this way?

> *There are different beliefs among Christians regarding whether we can expect to receive signs from God. There are Biblical examples where God honors a request for a sign (Gideon). But during the temptation of Jesus in the wilderness, the devil tempts him to throw himself off the temple and Jesus tells him it is not appropriate to put God to a test. (Matthew 4:7).*
>
> *God has given us minds and the ability to reason, along with His Word. Most of the time we can know whether we are acting in accordance with God's will by seeking His will in His Word. A life lived in continual stasis due to the need for a sign will be a life that denies the Word that God has given and the brains he has granted us. Pray to God and ask him for peace and direction. Those things will rarely come with a thunderclap such as Odysseus received from Zeus.*

DQ2: What quality do Eumaeus and Philoetius share with Odysseus' old dog, Argus? Does the Bible have anything to say about this quality? Look up Proverbs 21:21, Hosea 6:6, and John 15:13.

Loyalty to Odysseus is the quality they share with Argus.

Proverbs 21:21 says "He who pursues righteousness and loyalty finds life, righteousness and honor."

Hosea 6:6 says "For I delight in loyalty rather than sacrifice, and in the knowledge of God rather than burnt offerings.".

John 15:13 says "Greater love has no one than this, that one lay down his life for his friends."

God is faithful (loyal) to us. He expects loyalty and faithfulness from us. Eumaeus and Philoetius are good examples of virtue in this instance.

Chapter 14: The Slaying of the Suitors

Characters Introduced in this Chapter

Level C: Agelaus, Amphinomos, Medon, Phemius

Comprehension Questions and Answers

Q1: What does Odysseus do as soon as he reveals who he is?

Odysseus starts killing the suitors.

Q2: Who fights the suitors with Odysseus?

Fighting with Odysseus are his son, Telemachus, the shepherd, Eumaeus, and the cowherd, Philoetius.

Q3: Who tries to bring weapons to the suitors?

Melanthius, the goatherd, tries to bring weapons to the suitors.

Q4: How were four men able to slay over a hundred suitors?

Athene helped them. She caused the suitors' arrows to miss, and Odysseus and his allies' arrows to kill.

Q5: Why does Odysseus tell the minstrel to play happy music?

Odysseus wants to fool any passers-by into thinking that a happy feast is occurring. He knows that the kinsmen of the slain suitors will feel obliged to avenge their deaths and he wants to rest first.

Q6: What is unusual about Odysseus and Penelope's bed?

One of the bedposts is built from a living olive tree. The bed cannot be moved from the bedroom.

Q7: Draw a picture of a bed with a tree for one post, or make up your own unusual bed to draw.

Suggested Lines of Discussion to Pursue

DQ1: Did you think it was fair for Odysseus and the others to kill all the suitors? Wasn't there room for repentance?

Answers will vary. Some arguments for killing all of them might include that they had been infringing on Penelope's hospitality for years, that they were using up the resources of the kingdom in a bid for power and money, that they had plotted to kill Telemachus, and that they were trying to steal Odysseus' wife. Some arguments for not killing all of them might include an idea that they could have been defeated without being annihilated, that they could have been sorted into groups according to who was willing to swear to be loyal to Odysseus, and that killing is wrong.

DQ2: Why did Melanthius choose to arm the suitors?

Melanthius had taken the side of the suitors because he thought that one of them would one day be king and would favor him with money. The driving force behind his actions is personal gain. When he chooses to arm the suitors, it is because he thinks that arming them is the best way to save

his own life.

DQ3: Why doesn't Penelope believe Odysseus when he tells her

who he is?

Penelope has been waiting for Odysseus for nineteen years.

Knowing how much she longs for her husband, she is wary,

not wanting to be deceived. One of the gods could have

disguised himself (or herself) as Odysseus. A look-alike

could be trying to win her heart and Odysseus' throne. She

knows she has to be careful.

NOTE: The text says that Athene struck terror into the hearts of the

suitors with her "deadly aegis". The aegis of Zeus, sometimes used

by Athene, is usually depicted as a shield with the head of Medusa

on it. In other ancient texts it is the skin of a slain monster which

Zeus or Athene could wear over his or her garments.

Chapter 15: Peace in the Islands

Characters Introduced in this Chapter

      Level C: Dolius, Eupeithes

Map Work

      Level C: Sicily

Comprehension Questions and Answers

Q1: Where does Odysseus go in the morning?

      Odysseus goes to visit his father, Laertes.

Q2: Who rises up against Odysseus and his friends?

      The families of the suitors rise up to avenge their dead.

Q3: How is it that Odysseus and a few others can defeat such a crowd of angry armed men?

      Athene comes to their aid once again. She gives Laertes strength and guides his arrow, and then speaks aloud to the men of Ithaca and tells them not to fight.

Q4: How do the kinsmen of the suitors respond to Athene?

      They are terrified and run away.

Q5: What does Odysseus do? Why does he stop?

      Odysseus leaps to pursue the fleeing kinsmen. He stops because Zeus sends a thunderbolt down as a warning and because Athene advises him to stop.

Suggested Lines of Discussion to Pursue

DQ1: Several times, Odysseus has proven his identity with the scar of a serious injury on his leg. At the time he was injured as a child, Odysseus could not have predicted that such a wound would be useful to him. Have you ever had something bad happen, and then found out how God used it for good?

> *Answers will vary.*

> *Bring up the story of Joseph in Genesis. He was sold into slavery by his brothers, and then imprisoned unfairly. When his brothers come to him in fear and in need, he tells them that though they had intended evil toward him, God had intended good. Through his life in Egypt he was able to save the lives of his family as well as the lives of the Egyptians.*

DQ2: Discuss the concept of "home". What is home? How many different homes can a person have? What about a heavenly home?

> *For most children, "home" is where they live with their family. They can understand Odysseus' longing to go there. For older children and teens, "home" will have begun to take on new meaning. A home of their own. A spouse and children. A place where they are the authority figure. Discuss how a longing for that kind of home may be drawing them forward in their life, just as it drew Odysseus, against*

overwhelming odds, back to Ithaca. Sometimes people refer to "home" as their hometown. Home is the city or region where they grew up. The Bible also speaks of home as our heavenly dwelling (II Corinthians 5). Discuss the differences between the concepts of home. Which one draws them more? What do they long for when they picture their future, adult home? Their heavenly home?

Index of characters

Character	Chapter	Type	Level	Description
Achilles	5	demigod	C	Greatest Greek warrior.
Aeolus	3	human	B	Lord of the Winds.
Agamemnon	Pro	human	B	The High King of the Greeks. Slain upon his return from Troy.
Agelaus	14	human	C	Suitor of Penelope.
Ajax	5	human	C	Greek warrior who died at Troy.
Alcinous	9	human	C	King of Phaeacia.
Amphinomos	14	human	C	Suitor of Penelope.
Antinous	7	human		Suitor who plans to kill Telemachus.
Aphrodite	10	goddess	B	Goddess of love.
Apollo	1	god	B	Called "The Far Shooter". Maron was his priest.
Ares	10	god	B	God of war.
Arete	9	human	C	Queen of Phaeacia.
Argus	12	other	B	Odysseus' old dog.
Artemis	9	goddess	B	Goddess; called Artemis of the Crescent Moon.
Athene	7	goddess	A	Also called Pallas Athene. Goddess of wisdom.
Calypso	6	other	B	Nymph who takes in a shipwrecked Odysseus. In love with Odysseus.
Charybdis	6	other	A	Sea monster who sucks the sea into a whirlpool three times a day.
Circe	4	other	A	Beautiful witch who turns men into pigs.
Ctesippus	13	human	C	Suitor of Penelope.
Cyclopes	2	other	A	One-eyed giant monsters. Sons of Poseidon.

Character	Chapter	Type	Level	Description
Dolius	15	human	C	Husband of Laertes' housekeeper.
Echetus	13	human	C	Cannibal king.
Elpenor	5	human	C	Youngest sailor on Odysseus' ship.
Eumaeus	11	human	B	Odysseus' old swineherd.
Eupeithes	15	human	C	Father of Antinous.
Euryalus	10	human	C	Young man of Phaeacia who taunts Odysseus.
Eurycleia	7	human	B	Odysseus' and Telemachus' nanny.
Eurylochus	4	human	C	Kinsman and shipmate of Odysseus.
Eurymachus	12	human	C	Suitor of Penelope.
Eurynome	13	human	C	Housekeeper at the palace at Ithaca.
Hades	5	god	A	God who rules the underworld.
Helen	Pro	human	B	The Trojan war was fought over her.
Hermes	4	god	B	Messenger god. Called "Hermes of the Golden Rod".
Hyperion	5	god	C	The Sun Lord.
Ino	8	goddess	C	Sea goddess who rescues Odysseus from a storm.
Irus	12	human	C	Beggar who frequented the palace at Ithaca.
Laertes	2	human	C	Odysseus' father.
Laodamas	10	human	C	A prince of Phaeacia.
Maron	1	human	C	A Thracian priest of Apollo. Spared by Odysseus when he attacked Ismarus.
Maron's child	1	human	C	Maron's child. Spared by Odysseus.
Maron's wife	1	human	C	Maron's wife. Spared by Odysseus.
Medon	14	human	C	Herald in the palace of Ithaca.

Character	Chapter	Type	Level	Description
Melanthius	12	human	C	Royal goatherder in Ithaca.
Melantho	12	human	C	One of Penelope's maidens.
Menelaus	Pro	human	B	Helen's husband. King of Sparta who fought in the Trojan war.
Mentes	7	human	C	Odysseus' old friend. Athene takes on his form.
Minos	5	demigod	C	King with a golden scepter.
Nausicaa	9	human	B	Princess of Phaeacia. Finds Odysseus washed up on shore.
Nestor	7	human	C	Greek king who fought in the Trojan War.
Odysseus	Pro	human	A	King of Ithaca. Called "The Resourceful".
Odysseus' mother	5	human	C	Deceased mother of Odysseus.
Orion	5	demigod	C	Legendary hunter.
Paris	Pro	human	B	Prince of Troy. Stole Helen from Menelaus.
Penelope	5	human	A	Odysseus' wife.
Persephone	5	goddess	A	Hades' wife.
Phemius	14	human	C	Minstrel in the palace of Ithaca.
Philoetius	13	human	C	Cowherd at the palace at Ithaca.
Pisistratus	7	human	C	Nestor's son. Fought at Troy. Friend of Telemachus.
Polyphemus	2	other	C	Cyclops blinded by Odysseus.
Poseidon	2	god	A	God of the sea. Blue-haired.
Proteus	7	god	C	The "Old Man of the Sea".
Scylla	6	other	A	Six-headed monster who eats any large creature that passes by.
Sirens	6	other	A	Draw sailors to their deaths with their singing.

Character	Chapter	Type	Level	Description
Sisyphus	5	human	C	Imprisoned in the land of the dead, pushing a rock uphill for all eternity.
Tantalus	5	demigod	C	Imprisoned in the land of the dead, thirsting but unable to drink.
Telemachus	7	human	A	Odysseus' son.
Tiresias	5	human	B	Blind, dead prophet of Thebes.
Zeus	2	god	A	Chief god. Called "All-Father" and "Cloud Gatherer" and "The Lord of Thunder".

Map Work

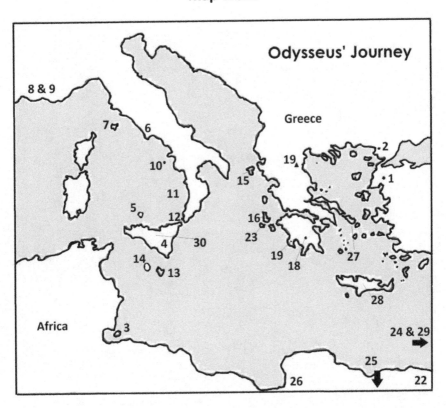

Odysseus' Journey

All Levels: Have students follow Odysseus' journey as they read the book. Numbers 1 through 16 trace his route.

Level C includes all places mentioned in the book. Numbers 17 through 30 comprise Level C.

Alphabetical List of Locations

# on Map	Place	Chapter	Level	Description
5	Aeolus' island	3	A	Home of Aeolus, Lord of the Winds. Called Aeolia.
20	Africa	7	A	Continent south of the Mediterranean Sea.
14	Calypso's Island	6	A	The island where Calypso lives.
7	Circe's Island	4	A	Circe's Island.
28	Crete	11	C	Island far from Ithaca.
24	Cyprus	7	C	Place Athene (as Mentes) tells Telemachus she is going.
27	Delos	9	C	Place where Artemis and Apollo were born.
22	Egypt	7	C	Place where fathers and sons sometimes shared kingship.
25	Ethiopia	7	C	Region in Africa whence Poseidon had gone.
17	Greece	Pro	A	Home of the city-states that fought against the Troy.
3	Island of the Lotus Eaters	1	A	Home of the lotus flower, whose fruit made men happy and ineffective.
2	Ismarus (Thrace)	1	A	A Thracian town close to the sea.
16	Ithaca	Pro	A	Greek city ruled by Odysseus
4	Land of the Cyclopes	2	A	Where the Cyclopes lived.
9	Land of the Dead	5	A	Hades: where people go after they die.
6	Land of the Giants	3	A	Place where giants destroyed 11 of the 12 ships.
26	Libya	7	C	Place on the north coast of Africa.

# on Map	Place	Chapter	Level	Description
8	Oceanus River	5	C	Girdles the earth and leads to the rivers of the dead.
19	Olympus	6	C	Mountain of the gods.
15	Phaeacia	9	A	Place where Odysseus washed ashore.
29	Phoenicia	7	C	A place Menelaus visited on his way home from Troy.
21	Pylos	7	C	Nestor was its king.
23	Same	7	C	"Bluffs of Same".
30	Sicily	15	C	Island in the Mediterranean.
10	Sirens' Island	6	A	Sirens sing their song from their island.
18	Sparta	Pro	C	Home of Menelaus
12	Strait of Scylla and Charybdis	6	A	Whirlpool in the sea.
13	Thrinacia	5	A	Island. Hyperion's cattle are there.
1	Troy	Pro	A	The location of the Trojan War
11	Wandering Rocks	6	A	Rocks not tethered to the sea floor. Apt to smash ships between them.

Relaxed Student Workbook Answer Key

Prologue
1. C
2. B
3. Greeks
4. A

Chapter 1
1. C
2. B
3. D
4. C
5. A
6. B
7. D

Chapter 2
1. C
2. Cyclopes,
   Poseidon
3. C
4. A
5. D
6. Nobody
7. C

Chapter 3
1. B
2. A
3. C
4. C
5. B
6. D

7. 11, 1
8. A

Chapter 4
1. Eurylochus
2. A
3. C
4. D

Chapter 5
1. B
2. C
3. D
4. C
5. A
6. B
7. C

Chapter 6
1. B
2. Singing
3. B
4. C
5. A
6. C
7. D
8. B
9. B
10. A

Chapter 7
1. A

2. C
3. D
4. A
5. C

Chapter 8
1. B
2. C
3. A
4. D
5. A
6. B
7. A

Chapter 9
1. D
2. C
3. C
4. City's edge;
      Palace;
      Father
5. B
6. A

Chapter 10
1. B
2. C
3. B
4. D
5. B
6. C
7. A

Chapter 11
1. C
2. C
3. B
4. D
5. C
6. B
7. A

Chapter 12
1. B
2. C
3. D
4. A
5. C
6. C

Chapter 13
1. B
2. D
3. B
4. C
5. B

Chapter 14
1. B
2. A
3. D
4. B
5. B
6. C
7. Answers will vary

Chapter 15
1. B
2. A
3. A
4. C
5. C

for more SneakerBlossom Study Guides please visit

sneakerblossom.com